### Read-About® Geography

# Appalachian Mountains

### By Jan Mader

**Consultant**
Nanci R. Vargus, Ed.D.
Assistant Professor of Literacy
University of Indianapolis, Indianapolis, Indiana

Children's Press®
A Division of Scholastic Inc.
New York   Toronto   London   Auckland   Sydney
Mexico City   New Delhi   Hong Kong
Danbury, Connecticut

Designer: Herman Adler Design
Photo Researcher: Caroline Anderson
The photo on the cover shows the Blue Ridge Mountains, North Carolina.

**Library of Congress Cataloging-in-Publication Data**

Mader, Jan.
  Appalachian Mountains / by Jan Mader.
    p. cm. – (Rookie read-about geography)
Includes index.
Summary: An introduction to the Appalachian Mountains, which run
through eighteen states.
  ISBN 0-516-22757-2 (lib. bdg.)          0-516-26834-1 (pbk.)
  1. Appalachian Mountains–Juvenile literature.  2. Appalachian
Mountains–Geography–Juvenile literature.  [1. Appalachian Mountains.]
I. Title.  II. Series.
  F106.M33 2004
  917.4–dc22

                                        2003016896

CHILDREN'S PRESS, and ROOKIE READ-ABOUT®,
and associated logos are trademarks and or registered trademarks
of Scholastic Library Publishing. SCHOLASTIC and associated logos
are trademarks and or registered trademarks of Scholastic Inc.
1 2 3 4 5 6 7 8 9 10 R 13 12 11 10 09 08 07 06 05 04

Which mountains stretch
all the way from Canada
to Alabama?

The Appalachian
Mountains do!

They run through
most of the eastern states.

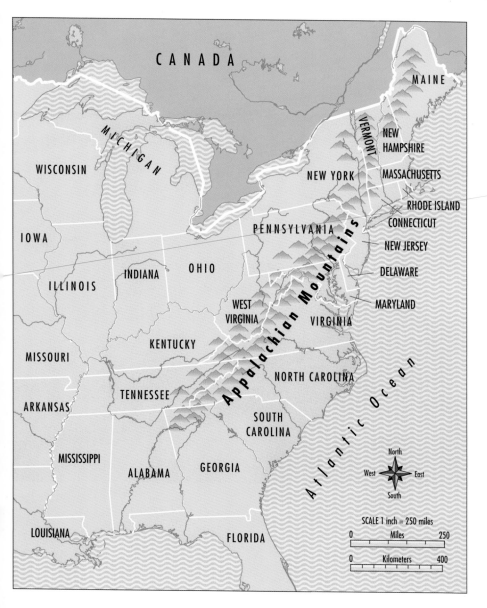

CANADA

MAINE

MICHIGAN

WISCONSIN

VERMONT

NEW HAMPSHIRE

NEW YORK

MASSACHUSETTS

RHODE ISLAND

CONNECTICUT

PENNSYLVANIA

NEW JERSEY

IOWA

INDIANA

OHIO

DELAWARE

ILLINOIS

WEST VIRGINIA

VIRGINIA

MARYLAND

Appalachian Mountains

MISSOURI

KENTUCKY

NORTH CAROLINA

Atlantic Ocean

TENNESSEE

ARKANSAS

SOUTH CAROLINA

MISSISSIPPI

GEORGIA

North

ALABAMA

West   East

LOUISIANA

South

FLORIDA

SCALE 1 inch = 250 miles

0   Miles   250

0   Kilometers   400

Mount Mitchell

Mount Mitchell is the highest mountain in the Appalachians.

It is in the Black Mountain Range. A range is a row of mountains.

The temperature and climate in the Appalachians changes with the elevation. Elevation is how high up you are.

Each season is different, too. In the winter, it can be cold and snowy.

In the spring, it can be rainy and cool. A storm may happen suddenly.

Summer in the Appalachian Mountains is warm.

The mountains are alive with plants, animals, and human visitors.

In the autumn, the trees turn red, orange, and yellow.

Thick forests cover the
Appalachian Mountains.
Fir trees grow high up in
the mountains.

Wildflowers, ferns, and mosses grow everywhere.

The Appalachian
Mountains have many
streams, waterfalls,
and rivers.

The Allegheny River
is one of the rivers. It
flows toward the west.

19

Bears

Bobcats, deer, and bears live in the Appalachian Mountains. Raccoons, skunks, and other small animals do, too.

Coal

Minerals such as iron ore, limestone, and coal can be found in the Appalachians.

Some people who live in the mountains are coal miners.

Other people are farmers. Farmers who live in the southern part of the Appalachians grow corn and tobacco.

Farmers who live in the northern part grow apples, barley, wheat, hay, and potatoes.

A farm

The Appalachian Trail is a famous path for walking in the mountains.

It is 2,168 miles long and passes through 14 states.

The Great Smoky Mountains National Park is in the Appalachians.

Many people visit this park each year and go hiking.

# Words You Know

Allegheny River

Appalachian Trail

autumn

bears

coal miner

fir trees

moss

Mount Mitchell

# Index

# About the Author

Jan Mader has been writing for children for over 15 years. Her natural curiosity and joy of life characterize her work. Jan and her family love to vacation in the mountains. Jan rides horses while her husband and sons go fishing. In fact, Jan can't think of any other place she'd rather be.

# Photo Credits

Photographs © 2004: Corbis Images: 26, 30 top right (Farrell Grehan), cover (David Muench); Dembinsky Photo Assoc.: 14, 30 bottom left (Adam Jones), 16, 20, 30 bottom right, 31 top right (Bill Lea), 22 (Patti McConville), 25 (Tod Patterson); Peter Arnold Inc.: 17, 31 bottom left (Matt Meadows), 10 (Phil Schermeister); Photo Researchers, NY: 19, 30 top left (Mark C. Burnett), 6, 31 bottom right (Will & Deni McIntyre), 23, 29, 31 top left (Kenneth Murray); Tim Barnwell Photography: 3, 9; Visuals Unlimited/Jeff Greenberg: 13.

Map by Bob Italiano